The Conflict Resolution Library™

Dealing with Competitiveness

• Don Middleton •

The Rosen Publishing Group's
PowerKids Press™
New York

This book is dedicated to my wife, Sue; my daughters, Jody and Kim; my mother-in-law, Mim; and my parents, Bernice and Helmut Bischoff. Also, special thanks to authors and friends Diana Star Helmer and Tom Owens for believing in me. —Don Middleton

Published in 1999 by The Rosen Publishing Group, Inc.
29 East 21st Street, New York, NY 10010

Photo Credits and Photo Illustrations: p. 4 © Bill Tucker/International Stock; p. 7 © Arthur Tilley/FPG International; p. 8 © Steve Jones/FPG International; p. 11 © Michael Paras/International Stock; p. 12 © George Ancona/International Stock; pp. 15, 19 © Bill Tucker/International Stock; p. 16 by Seth Dinnerman; p. 20 © Patrick Ramsey/International Stock.

First Edition

Layout and design: Erin McKenna

Middleton, Don.
    Dealing with competitiveness / by Don Middleton.
            p.   cm.—(The conflict resolution library)
    Includes index.
    Summary: Explains competition, what it is, its importance, and how to be a good winner as well as a good loser.
    ISBN 0-8239-5267-3
    1. Competition (Psychology) in children—Juvenile literature.
    [1. Competition (Psychology)] I. Title. II. Series.
    BF723.C6M53 1998
    302'14—dc21   98-22633
                                                                        CIP
                                                                         AC

Manufactured in the United States of America

Contents

Competition

Competition (KOM-peh-TIH-shun) is trying our hardest to be the best at something. At school, we may compete in a spelling bee or for a part in a school play. When we compete, somebody often wins while another person loses. It's okay to lose. Maybe you will win next time. The important thing is to be proud of yourself for doing your best.

Competition helps us improve at something. It helps people discover what we can do when we try our hardest.

◀ It feels good to try your best at things.

Learning Through Competition

You will probably find that you are very good at some sports and **activities** (ak-TIH-vih-teez) and not as good at others. But you can always **improve** (im-PROOV) your skills with practice and hard work. You might also need help from others to improve at something.

Try your best at whatever you're doing. Be proud when you do well. Try to learn how you might do better in the future.

Extra help from a coach or teacher can help you improve at something. ▶

Two Sisters

Jane was studying at the kitchen table. Her older sister, Andrea, sat down next to her. "Can I help you with your math homework?" Andrea asked.

"Thanks. It's hard for me to learn new things in math. You're lucky math is so easy for you," Jane said.

"Math may be easy for me, but you're better at spelling," Andrea replied.

Siblings (SIH-blings) may compete and find out that they are better at different things.

◀ When people are good at something, they can help another person improve.

Competing Against Others

We all compete against others. We try our hardest to win a softball game. We play the piano the best we can at a music competition. These are healthy kinds of competition. If we didn't try our best at these things, there wouldn't be any reason to play.

Sometimes competing against others can go too far. Some people cheat to make sure they win. That's not fair. In healthy competition, winning isn't the only thing that matters. What matters is that we all try our best.

It's a good idea to practice before a competition. ▶

Jeff and Tom

After school, Jeff and Tom hurried to change into their gym clothes. Tryouts for the track team were being held today. "I'm sure we'll both make the team," Tom said as he tied his running shoes.

"I hope so. But I also hope we don't have to race against each other," Jeff said.

"Even if we do, and one of us beats the other, we're still friends, right?" Tom asked.

"Right! Hey, let's just try our best," Jeff answered as he followed Tom outside.

◀ People can compete for sports teams or other clubs and still be friends.

Poor Winners

Everyone likes to win. Winning makes us feel good about ourselves. Our friends and families know how much we have practiced. They cheer for us when we win. But some people are poor winners. These people try to make the losing person or team members feel bad. A real winning team knows how to thank the other team for playing a good game and for being good sports. This lets the losing team know that the winning team cares about their feelings.

It's okay to be happy when you win. Just remember the other team's feelings too. ▶

Poor Losers

When you compete, you agree to play by the rules. Part of playing by the rules is losing **gracefully** (GRAYS-fuh-lee). After losing, everyone feels **disappointed** (dis-uh-POYN-ted). You might cry because you're so upset. That's okay. But it's important to lose without getting angry. Think about how you did and how you can do better next time. Tell the winners they played a good game. It's hard to lose, but be a good sport. People will **respect** (rih-SPEKT) you for it.

◀ Losing a game can make you feel sad. But try to learn from the loss so that you will improve.

Scared to Fail

Some people are afraid of losing. It's okay to be afraid. But don't let that fear stop you from competing or from trying your best. A great way to lower your fear is to practice. The more you practice, the better you will perform. Soon you may find yourself on the winning team. If you never compete, you never give yourself the chance to win or to improve your skills. Losing lets you know that you need a bit more practice.

You'll get better at a skill if you practice often. ▶

The Chess Club

Larry and Chris had been talking about joining the school chess club. "Chess club starts in ten minutes," Larry said.

"I don't think I have time," Chris said. He was afraid of not doing well.

Larry said, "Come on. You said you'd do it."

"Okay," said Chris. "Maybe I'll try it once."

After chess club, Larry said, "You did well."

"Maybe I'll come back," Chris said, smiling. He was proud of himself for trying.

◄ You won't know if you're good at something until you give it a try.

Be a Good Sport

Being in a competition can be very exciting. With lots of **concentration** (kon-sen-TRAY-shun), your mind and your body work as a team to help you do your very best. Knowing that you played your best will make you feel good, whether your team wins or loses. If you are on the winning side, be a good winner. If things didn't go your way, be a good sport.

Don't forget to have fun. Having fun is part of competition too!

Glossary

activity (ak-TIH-vih-tee) A thing to do, such as sewing or running.

competition (KOM-peh-TIH-shun) A game, contest, or race.

concentration (kon-sen-TRAY-shun) Focusing your thoughts and attention on one thing.

disappointed (dis-uh-POYN-ted) To feel let down.

gracefully (GRAYS-fuh-lee) Politely or kindly.

improve (im-PROOV) To get better at something.

respect (rih-SPEKT) To think highly of someone.

sibling (SIH-bling) A person's sister or brother.

Index